Pane Andov

THE QUICKEST WAY TO DEVELOP EXTRASENSORY PERCEPTION

**REMOTE VIEWING - CLAIRVOYANCE - SECOND SIGHT
TRAINING MANUAL**

Pure Tranquility Publishing

Copyright © Pure Tranquility Publishing 2019

Website: www.puretranquilitypublishing.com

Email: puretranquillitypublishing@gmail.com

Published 2019

TABLE OF CONTENT

Table of content 5

The Author 6

Introduction 11

Remote Viewing 12

Clairvoyance 23

Stage One 27

Stage Two 33

Stage Three 38

Stage Four 41

Stage Five 44

Stage Six 47

Stage Seven 53

Conclusion 59

THE AUTHOR

Pane Andov is an Australian citizen born in Skopje, Macedonia in 1973.

In 1980, during a walk with his older brother Milance Andov, his life took an unusual turn after experiencing a Close Encounter of the Fourth Kind. They were both mesmerized by the sight of an approaching alien flying craft emanating strong yellow, orange, and red pulsating light.

After getting within a distance of fewer than fifty meters, the object released a very powerful flash of bright light. In less than a few seconds, they both realized that somehow they have been teleported inside the alien craft.

The author was not hurt in any way by the alien beings, but they did run some tests, and when the tests came back satisfactory, they incited a procedure that increased his brain capacity. In some strange way, Andov felt that they were rewiring his brain; putting in some kind of connection so they will know where he is at all times and in case of an emergency they would be able to protect him from the "Others".

Most important, Andov was told that they have altered his DNA functionality so he could experience and understand certain things.

Both the author and his brother were missing for about two hours.

After the author and his brother were returned home, Andov started manifesting telepathic abilities and having spontaneous out of body experiences.

Not long after, an unpleasant incident occurred with his mother, Jozefina Andova, which resulted in little Andov being forced to stop using those abilities. The entire Close Encounter of the Fourth kind is published in Volume 3 of "The Awakening" series.

In 1988, inspired by his uncle Rudek Mozar, he became interested in all kinds of paranormal phenomena, Ancient civilizations, Transcendental Meditation, Astral projection, Tai Chi, Kriya Yoga, and Esoteric Buddhism.

Of all, Andov was most fascinated by Astral projection. He remembered everything that happened to him in 1980 and that he had already experienced a few short spontaneous out of body experiences, but he couldn't tell anyone about it. For his mother, this was a sensitive subject, so the author tried to avoid talking about the 1980 UFO event, as much as possible.

Another reason why he kept quiet was also that in the 1980s, UFOs and aliens were still a taboo in the Balkan region. Anyone who talked about this subject or claimed that they had been contacted or abducted by aliens, would soon end up without friends or worse.

Feeling an unexplained hunger for knowledge, young Andov started reading all of the books and magazines that he could get his hands on that covered the topics of his interest.

Around 1989, Andov felt that he had enough theoretical input, and he started pushing the training very hard. Thus, among other daily training whose purpose was mostly for the development of chi energy and achieving extrasensory perception, Andov also started practicing a combination of Nidra and Kriya Yoga.

He used to either sit in the lotus position for hours or simply lay flat in a "Shavasana" position, entering a deep Trance and constantly attempting to depart his body by his own will.

It was 21 April 1990 when he finally achieved his first self-induced out of body experience. That breakthrough, gave him the additional motivation to start pushing even harder. Every new out of body experience was longer, more fascinating and more mysterious.

Andov simply fell in love with astral traveling and 27 years later, he is still an astral traveler. In time his abilities increased to such a level, that he was able to stay out of his physical body for hours, fully conscious.

Sometimes he was out of his body for more than eight hours without any loss of awareness and clear astral perception. The new and mysterious world that was opening in front of him, made him realize that reality was not what it seemed to be, but something completely different.

The author recalls that as soon as he managed to reach Earth's orbit with his astral body, he started seeing UFOs constantly going in and out of the planet. Out of curiosity, Andov started following some of the UFOs to see where they were going and what they were doing.

Most of them were either hovering or slowly moving inside thunderstorms, others were simply disappearing into the Oceans, while some were directly flying into active volcanoes. But it those who were hovering over houses and buildings in the populated areas that caught Andov's attention.

One thing leads to another and in time he saw enough to understand that some UFOs are not just violating human privacy, but also taking humans without any given consent and doing things to them that are difficult to explain, even in a book, without causing emotional trauma.

Many times Andov witnessed a fight between UFOs. Most of the time there was no winners but sometimes a UFO was completely disintegrated. In the beginning, it appeared to him as though these conflicts were only a fight for dominance, but later he found out that not all alien beings are hostile towards humans, neither do they agree with the manipulative behavior of the abusive ones.

Rapidly, he began to understand that humanity is under constant surveillance and exploitation by a few extraterrestrial species. He started researching and he found out that the highest levels of NASA, US Navy, NSA, and CIA, have been briefed and are fully aware of the extraterrestrial presence here on Earth.

However the so-called, Shadow Government that funds and controls all of them, has chosen to keep the truth hidden from the general population. Andov never stopped studying the moves of the Shadow Government regarding the alien question.

One by one, the missing pieces of the mosaic started to fall into place and he was starting to see a bigger picture of what was going on.

In parallel to his adventures on the Astral Plane, Andov led a normal and productive life. Andov graduated in 1992 in Skopje - High Voltage Systems. He started his career in 1993 in Macedonian Telecom and worked on Power Supply Systems.

He further specialized in computer software connected to Uninterruptible Power Supply. After 12 years, he left the company after realizing that computer software and the advancement of Power Supply Systems, were not his life objectives.

Together with his wife, Andov began to direct his time and energy towards making a difference by way of sharing new information and a new understanding of the strange reality we live in, in his birth country Macedonia. Their method of creating public conscious awareness was via a monthly publication of their own magazine, which they called "The Sixth Sense".

After publishing thirty-two issues of the magazine, a difference in public awareness began to manifest. This created a collective change amongst peoples' lives indicated by a very high number of replies received with gratitude, for the provided information.

As the Chief Editor of the magazine, it gave Pane unrestricted rights to document information regarding; ancient civilizations, UFO phenomena, Top Secret military projects, HAARP, Secret Societies and Illuminati, various types of meditation, studies about kundalini energy, astral projection, remote viewing, telepathy, aura's, clairvoyance, psychometrics, psychokinesis and much more.

In 2007, Andov published his first book "Extraordinary Powers in Humans". Among very effective training programs, specially chosen and designed for spiritual self-development, the book offered 18 of the author's astral trips describing his contacts with alien species as the dominant subject.

After moving to Melbourne, Australia in 2009 with his family, Andov gained further qualifications in the area of Graphic Pre-press from Cambridge International College. After gaining his qualifications he again started working in the field of Telecommunications.

He spent the next 3 years working for a Subcontractor of TELSTRA - Australia's leading provider of mobile phones, home phones, and broadband Internet.

Not long after, together with his family, he moved to Gold Coast, on the East Coast of Australia, where they currently reside. During his life, Andov gained vast technical experience, which in total includes 15 years in Telecommunications and 4 years in Technical Administration.

However, he never considered his technical background as his biggest asset, but his knowledge and experience in the science of Psionics.

Andov is a man of many talents.

In parallel with his technical profession, he is also an author, public speaker and instructor of Psionic arts. Over the years, Andov's teachings were received by thousands of students worldwide. His teachings are mostly in the fields of Kundalini Yoga, remote viewing, controlled out of body experience, Extrasensory Perception, and Second Sight.

Back in 2008, he was the organizer of the Global Healing Meditations when thousands of participants were meditating together worldwide.

The purpose of the Global Healing Meditation was to unite and transform the transmitted psionic energy of so many people into one powerful stream of healing energy that would heal and raise the vibration of planet Earth.

Andov is the author of "The Awakening – Life Force Energy", "The Awakening – Key to Extraterrestrial Messages", "The Quickest Way To Develop Extrasensory Perception", "Extraordinary Powers in Humans", "Dimensional Gateways – A Practical Guide to Astral Projection", "Alien Implants – Hacking the Alien Internet", "The Paranormal Aspects of Crop Circles - Deciphering the Alien Code", "Someone else is on the Moon: Fake Apollo landings and alien bases on the moon", "Alien presence confirmed: We Are Not In Control", "Saturn: The secrets of the extraterrestrial engineers" and few other books.

His vision is still one and the same – not to escape Earth, but to bring heaven to Earth...

INTRODUCTION

It is author's understanding that the life force itself is coming from higher dimensions of the Universe, through a medium called Psionic medium.

This medium, also known as Psionic Field, stands for the infinitive ocean of divine energetic substance that runs throughout the entire Universe. Planet Earth, as the entire solar system, as the entire galaxy, the cluster and the supercluster, is connected with this gigantic Psionic Field.

Andov has spent a life time searching and experimenting for effective ways how human consciousness can access this Psionic Field. With over 30,000 out of body experiences, thousands of hours of remote viewing experimentation and years of blindfold ESP training, the author is presenting a functional meditation method that allows the human consciousness to penetrate into the Psionic Field.

A complete overview of the Remote Viewing (RV) process is given and how it can be utilized by the consciousness to its fullest. This Psionic Field stretches throughout all seven Planes of existence, via a gigantic energy network. The author fully explains that at the beginning stage of the RV, the observation and the extraction of information is limited only to the Etheric Plane of existence, but in time, as the training stage progresses, the student becomes capable of taking a step further by replacing the RV with a direct projection of the consciousness into the Astral Plane. The density of a certain dimension of existence is important. Out of the seven dimensions that exist in the Universe, the Astral dimension is the third lowest on the scale, with the Physical dimension being the densest.

With the help of the astral projection new horizons are opening up to us, showing us that death as such do not exist, and that it is only a transition of the consciousness from the physical into the immaterial world. For anyone who is willing to make a serious effort and few years of intensive training, this book contains all the necessary instructions how one can reach a point of ESP development that will provide a solid access to immaterial part of the Universe and become an active participant in the global process of Awakening.

REMOTE VIEWING

Remote viewing is a term in Parapsychology that describes a process in which the psychically gifted person is watching some kind of astral television based on a program that he/she has chosen on his/her own.

This process enables a well-trained remote viewer to focus on his/her mental screen where psychic visions start to appear and the viewer uses mental efforts to catch those psychic pictures, which in fact are astral reflections of places that he/she wants to observe.

This ability is actually related to the human's third eye that makes it possible for the mind to see things that are not visible to physical eyes.

Therefore, the simple definition of remote viewing would be - observing the physical, etheric and the astral area without leaving the physical body. However, many anomalies that can distort much of the results of the remote viewing might appear in the early stages of the development of this extraordinary ability. That's because a beginner strongly focusing on scanning some area is unable to hold his/her mind unattached longer, and often becomes emotionally attached to his/her individual feelings and opinions concerning the things he or she is watching.

Those individual feelings and opinions will have major influence on the already very weak astral reflections of the chosen area, and it will distort them or even trigger observation of some other area, which suits mostly his/her suppressed desires.

Therefore, a student on the start line must learn to shut down his/her own personal feelings and attitudes first if he/she wants to succeed mastering the remote viewing ability. One should become an empty receiver to be able to absorb major amount of data, classify them, filter or analyze them. In other words, once one succeeds to catch the astral radiation of the target area, he/she has to remember them and analyze them later. Later the student will learn another approach to the analysis.

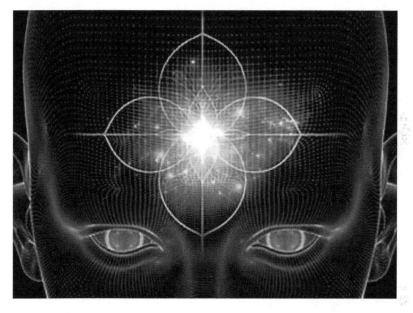

All this etheric and astral radiation that streams through the mental screen is provided by the third eye and projected directly to the mind.

Any invisible physical place becomes visible for the third eye if the mind succeeds to dive deep into the etheric or the astral matter and remains there long enough. Nevertheless, as I mentioned before, the etheric and the astral plane are almost infinite areas full of infinite radiation.

Thus, in the beginning, the mental screen of the remote viewer is flooded with hundreds of other reflections coming from those planes in the shape of psychic pictures or visions. Anyway, practice has shown that as far as the radiation that appears on the remote viewer's mental screen is concerned, I am positive that mostly it has its origin in the astral plane and much rarely in the etheric plane.

I know it sounds contradictory, and logically it should be the other way around, but the fact is, it is the truth. It is simple, because our third eye absorbs the sensitive images that come from the astral plane filled with thoughts better than the ones that come from the etheric plane mostly filled with vital energy.

However, every student must understand clearly that remote viewing is ability hard to achieve and that it will take some time before one is capable of selecting the target astral reflection from the infinite number of other astral reflections appearing on the mental screen. Thus, in the beginning, one's mind must become a clear mental surface open to all the astral radiation coming from the astral area.

Then, by using the third eye one must learn how to focus the mind on chosen targets and block all other images visible to him/her. This is a hard period for every student, but in time and with practice it can be achieved.

Long ago, I personally had some difficult time mastering it and I will try to explain how the whole thing works:

Before the student even tries to achieve the remote viewing, first of all he/she must learn to create mental shapes, forms and images of the places in the mind helped by the ability of visualization and concentration. Then, the student must learn how to keep them frozen for as long as he/she wants to, not letting them disappear from the mental screen.

Therefore, at the very beginning of the mental creation process, the observer must become capable of holding the selected target in his/her imagination. To achieve that, drawing the place on a sheet of paper for at least 30 times, and practicing the visualization of the place for at least 7 days for about 10-15 minutes would help a lot. That would help the observer to "imprint" the picture of the selected area deep in the etheric matter below the astral plane.

Anyway, after a few days of previous visualization exercises, the student should sit in some comfortable half lying or lying position, in some quiet place where he/she can work in peace and silence. The potential remote viewer should close the eyes and start to observe the mental screen. At this stage, the viewer does not have to imagine or force a mental creation of some kind, but to become a passive observer. The effect that will follow will be very similar to watching a movie in the cinema. The only difference is that this time the screen will be in his/her head.

The secret lies in becoming a silent witness, without getting emotionally attached to things that will start appearing on the mental screen. In time, the astral reflections will start to enter the mind and the remote viewer has to put some mental effort to remember them.

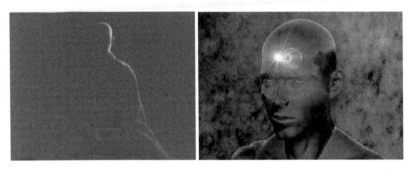

The training with the zener cards (which will be mentioned further on in this eBook) can also help the student activate the mental screen. Besides the zener training, a constant focus on looking straight up with eyes closed can also trigger the awakening of the third eye (Ajna chakra), and because of that, the mental screen will become more visible.

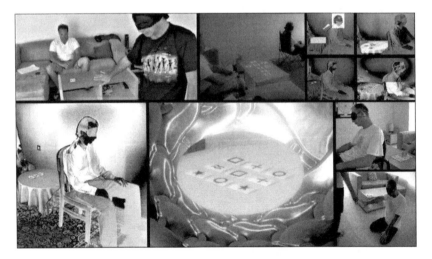

In the beginning, in front of the student's eyes only total blackness will be visible, which in time will become foggy, and then as the third eye becomes more and more awaken, it will become an open mental screen where the astral pictures will be coming. It is interesting to mention that the third eye is the one doing all the work and the mind is only the boss in the whole process.

Anyway, it is not necessary for the student to visualize the third eye becoming shiny or to take some shape like circle, triangle, etc., only to remain a passive witness of the astral visions streaming into his/her mind.

Here how the blackness is altered by the open mental screen:

From the depth of the blackness of the mental screen slowly but surely, some unclear figures and contours will start to appear.

In time, the student will notice an unclear picture appearing and it will be gone in a split of a second.

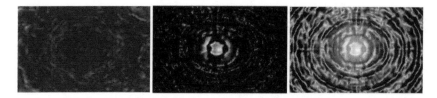

Then, if the student's mind remains calm and only focused on the mental screen without any emotional attachment other pictures will come. The color of the pictures will be unclear and mostly black and white in the beginning, and as the time passes by, images will become clearer and somewhat colorful.

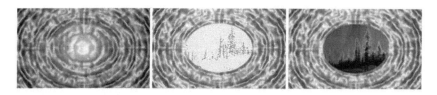

The duration of these astral pictures will vary and it will be determined by the student's will to hold them or reject them on the mental screen.

Later, when the remote viewer reaches an advanced level of psychic observation, the pictures will have clear colors.

When the student reaches this level of development, he/she will start to hear sounds in the mind connected to the related astral vision almost instantly.

Eventually, the pictures and the sounds will become perfectly clear to the observer.

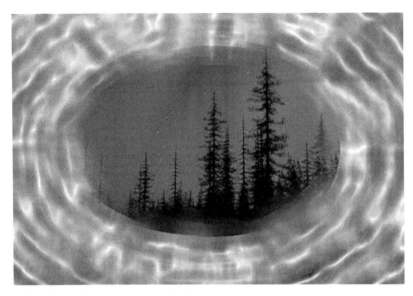

When that starts to happen, the student will know he/she has reached the point where from he/she can try to find the selected target of the carefully chosen place. The whole process at this stage will appear as somebody presenting the student infinite series of pictures of people, animals, close and distant places, houses, buildings, space images, underwater images, pictures from another time, etc. In time and with practice, those pictures will become motion pictures.

Thus, the remote viewer faces another task and he/she has to learn how to freeze the chosen picture, and analyze it without vanishing from the mental screen. The analyzing process should be done strictly mentally and without using words in the thoughts and with no emotional response towards the astral picture; otherwise, the picture will vanish from the mental screen. It is not advisable to even think in pictures because that will surely influence the sensitive mental screen.

If the remote viewer is capable of reaching this point of observation, I suggest a further try for observing the astral radiation by using a higher level of consciousness. By a higher level of consciousness, I mean consciousness of the consciousness itself.

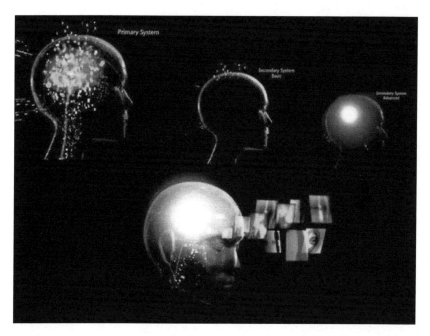

One consciousness exists in the average consciousness, and observes filters and analyzes all the data coming and leaving the remote viewer's mental screen.

In other words, the remote viewer adapts to this new part of the consciousness and when this is achieved, the viewer can easily think and make choices in a higher and subtler way not touching the sensitive astral pictures. Then, all that needs to be done is to focus on the selected area and in a few seconds, it will become visible for the remote viewer.

Once the viewer catches the astral radiation of the target area, he/she can easily move and observe everywhere and everything just by using a small mental effort. Here is one example of how the remote viewing process is done: Let us assume that a picture of a large apartment appears on the mental screen of the student.

To succeed with the remote observation of the apartment, the student should use some mental efforts to partly enter the mental screen by pulling the picture towards the third eye.

While this process is on, the remote viewer's mind must remain maximally calm and under no circumstances to become emotionally attached to the picture, because if it does, the picture will be altered by another one more suitable to his/her emotional charge.

The next step is to locate the astral reflection of the target and to "freeze" the picture on the mental screen.

Once the student succeeds that, he/she has to pull the picture closer to the third eye using strong mental efforts to slip into the picture at the same time.

In other words, the student has to magnetically pull the picture in and to use mental efforts to push him/herself out and walk through the picture at the same time.

The whole secret at this stage is in the balance of these two forces – the outer, which one pulls towards him/herself and the inner, which he/she forces out.

In this particular case, one has to pull the picture of the entrance room of the selected apartment towards the dot between the physical eyes, and walk through the entrance of the apartment visible on the mental screen at the same time.

Once the student succeeds to pull that off, he/she is free to observe the other rooms in the apartment.

In the beginning, the remote viewer will face certain problems moving in some direction. In most cases, if the moving procedure is not done correctly, it will transport the observation to a completely new place.

The trick is, the student who has chosen to move (for example) to the right in the apartment has to start pulling the appropriate movement towards the third eye and simultaneously push the consciousness to move right.

That will surely lead to the biolocation of the consciousness, and that is why the remote viewer has to stay in the middle point between the apartment and the mental screen.

If the bilocation is too weak, it will not be perceived as it should be and if it is too strong, it will induce an astral projection in the apartment.

Because of the fact that the main purpose of the remote viewing is to observe distant places without leaving the physical body, the student must be capable of holding the mind helped by the third eye no further than the mental screen. The mind of the remote viewer must be neither too shallow nor too deep. The perfect location of the mind would be very little out of the surface line of the mental screen towards the apartment, and constantly on alert not to go deeper.

However, if that is too difficult for a student, he/she can simply lock the mind on the surface line of the mental screen, and the observation will be just fine. The remote viewing process will run smoothly, but the ability of moving will be little reduced. All the experiences that the remote viewer manages to collect from the selected area should be put in a diary.

That has many purposes, but one of them is adapting the consciousness to the etheric and astral vibrations, which will allow the remote viewer to be constantly aware of the other planes while still on the physical plane. In time, a well-trained remote viewer will be capable of observing distant places on the mental screen with small mental efforts with unbelievable accuracy and precision.

What is most interesting, after a few years of remote viewing practice, one will be able to observe the physical, etheric and astral area just by closing his/her eyes while enjoying a ride on the bus, resting, drinking coffee or doing some everyday job. That will surely bring a complete expansion of the remote viewer's consciousness in which he/she will be constantly sensitive to an even tiniest radiation coming from the etheric or the astral world. From this point of psychic development on, there are no real limits for the human consciousness.

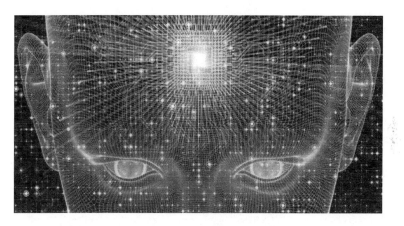

By using this method of achieving the extraordinary ability known as remote viewing, very soon you will become capable of observing distant places helped by your third eye with major precision without leaving your physical body.

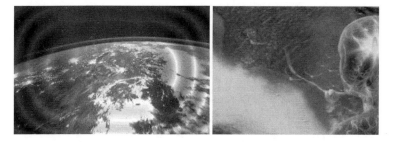

While you will be using your physical eyes to see the world around your physical body, you will be using your third eye to see much deeper into the Universe. Please, use your new ability wisely and do not ever use it for selfish reasons.

CLAIRVOYANCE

Clairvoyance is a paranormal ability closely tied with the remote viewing. The human's third eye has the leading role since it enables the mind to see through the mental screen. There are many methods to develop the third eye. I have chosen to present the method I have mastered a long time ago and am completely sure it works.

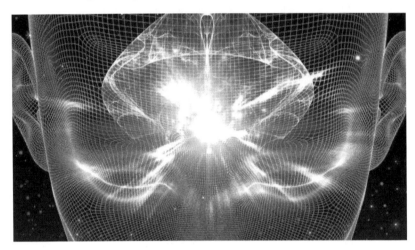

The method is universal and most of the psychic abilities can be developed through it. This method, which in fact is a system of exercises, consists of seven stages starting with the zener cards and as each stage is completed, the training gets harder and harder.

However, before I go any deeper into the subject of the psychic training, it is better to clear up some things first concerning the zener cards. The zener cards, also known as ESP cards, are the basis of the modern parapsychology. Although most people consider them just a useful tool for ESP testing, they are much more than that. The use of the zener cards is also a powerful tool through which individuals can awake and develop their third eye with a special training. One deck of the zener cards consists of five symbols multiplied five times - star, waves, plus, circle and square.

All of the 25 cards are totally black on one side and on the other side there is white background with bolded black colored symbol. In the beginning, the task of the student helped by an inner sense is to feel or see the symbol on the card. Because during the training the student is blindfold, while the sense of the student's physical sight is off, the other senses increase and sharpen more. However, the purpose of this universal method is not to sharpen the other senses, but to awake and develop a (figuratively speaking) "new sense", which contains the other five senses in it and much more.

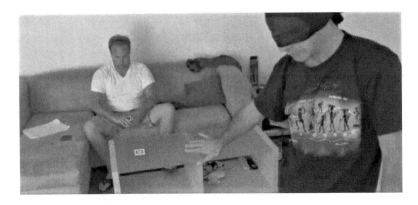

It is completely irrelevant how you call this new sense – third eye, sixth sense or Ajna chakra. You will not make a mistake, because it is the same thing. Once this new sense starts to awake, most of the psychic powers can be achieved, cultivated and made ready for everyday use.

The system of exercises to follow will lead you to a point where you will become the master or your mental potentials.

The universal method is so complete that each of you willing to sacrifice about two or three years of your life can achieve higher mental powers and develop your psychic abilities beyond words.

Nevertheless, although some authors promise you that you will develop your psychic powers in weeks by some specific method, I will not give promises like that and I will give you only the time that took me to develop them. It must become perfectly clear to every true student that it takes major self-discipline, top determination and persistence to keep up with the everyday hard training.

STAGE ONE

As for almost everything else in psychic practice, the student must find a quiet and isolated place to be able to work undisturbed with an assistant. It must be done in pairs because the student must be blindfold all the time during the training, and will need somebody to put the zener cards behind him/her and inform the student about the accuracy of the answers. Sometimes a group training sessions are also very efficient, but at the beginning the best results are achieved if the student is alone with the trainer, so he/she can unleash and focus his/her psionic energy so to speak, uninterrupted by other thoughts and energies.

The whole process in this stage works like this:

The blindfold student must sit on a chair and the assistant should sit two meters behind him and put the cards one by one on a smaller table. In the beginning, there must be some clear space between the student and the table where the zener cards with the symbol up will be put.

Since it is going to take about two to three hours of practicing, some instrumental music cannot do any harm to the training process and it will provide a smoother training. However, it is important that the music is with relatively slow rhythm and pleasant for hearing. Some sounds from the ambient or New Age music enjoyable to both of them will do just fine. However, the quiet and slow instrumental music can bring only benefit to the training and if somebody likes to practice in silence, it is perfectly OK, and can work in silence.

The assistant should reshuffle the deck well, and put the cards one by one. The table, except for the only one card, which has to be put in the middle point, must be completely clear of any other objects. For now, the side with the symbol of the card should be up because it will allow the student to feel or see it more easily. If during the process of practicing, the assistant forgets to remove the deck from the table, it will be a major mistake. The rest of the cards in the deck, though turned on the side with the black background up, will surely influence the student's efforts to locate the symbol of the target card, which is in the middle of the table.

For that reason, the assistant who can seat on a comfortable sofa should split the deck in three piles. All those parts should be put on the sofa and by no excuse on the table where the target card is. The first pile should contain the wrong answers, the second the correct answers and the third one normally, the cards which remain to be put on the table.

When the mental scan of all cards of the deck is over, the assistant informs the student of the correct answers and notes the result in a notebook, which can be used for monitoring the student's progress.

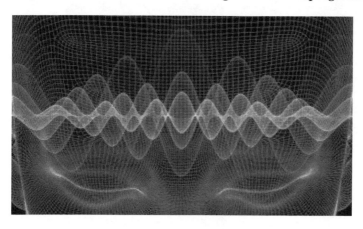

Then, the assistant has to reshuffle the deck well and when that is done, the process goes on with the next deck of cards. The student is allowed only one answer, and the assistant (at least in this stage of the training) should confirm the result of the student's answer with a simple Yes/No, or True/False.

The black fold around the student's eyes should be neither too tight, nor too feeble. Student's clothes should be comfortable like tracksuit or so, to be able to sit in the chair for hours without feeling uncomfortably.

Before the training starts, it is advisable to try to sit in one position on the chair that mostly suits the student's body and to "freeze" in that position. The student can put his/her arms on the knees or thighs, but he/she should try to hold the head, neck and spine in straight line as much as possible. Until now, I have explained the basic rules of the training, and now I will explain the inner procedure to be performed in the mind. The inner process, which will be performed in the student's mind, requires great ability of visualization, concentration, and focus on the inner psychic force and by all means great ability of the consciousness to move out of the physical body.

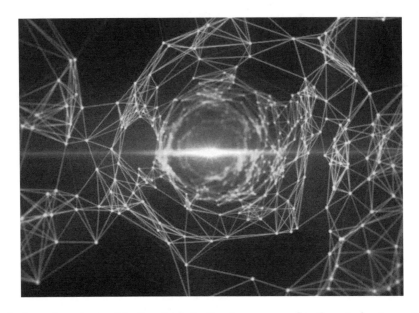

Before the start with the first deck of zener cards, the student must calm the mind by entering peaceful meditative state. After having calmed his/her thoughts and reached inner peace, the student should concentrate on the inner energy, which flows through his/her body.

When the student feels the streaming of pleasant bioenergy, he/she is ready for the training and can give the assistant a sign to put the first card on the table. Then, the student must completely free his/her mind and to try to pull out the inner sense, which lies deep down in him/her to feel the objects that are around.

The first thing the student must concentrate on is the streaming of the energy between him/her and the chair. The student has to feel the chair as a part of him/her the way a driver feels the car while driving it.

Then, he/she should redirect the psychic feeling following the pattern: – between him/her and the carpet (if there is any); between him and the legs of the table; the whole table; the target card; and at the end between him/her and the card's symbol.

The secret lies in establishing some kind of emotional bridge between one's self and the symbol of the target card.

The rest will come by itself.

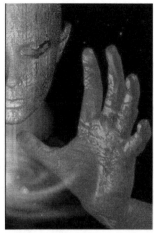 

The establishing of this kind of an emotional bridge should be done very slowly and with no rush because it will produce contra effect if done otherwise. In other words, the student should not keep a feeling of impatience within since it will surely lead to a wrong answer. On the contrary, the correct answer comes as a result of patient psychic touch between the student and the symbol of the card.

In time and with practice, the student will surely reach the level of being capable to easily move his/her psychic touch onto the objects that are around.

The inner feeling will develop greatly and it will become so sharp that sometimes the student will feel almost equal as a physical touch with the card. After the student reaches 70% of accuracy in the answers, he/she should repeat this score with the next five decks.

Note: Under no condition, no matter how well the training goes, it is not advisable for the student at this stage to start working with two cards at the same time. That would be a big mistake, which will cost the student much more than he/she can imagine. If the student tries to feel two or more cards in the same time, he/she will soon lose the psychic touch and will have to work very hard again to reach the same point of development.

In other words, the student will lose two months of training just in a few minutes and will have to practice even longer to reach the same level of accuracy. Please, believe my words, because I have passed the whole training myself and encountered the same problem.

The practice with more cards will follow in the next stages when the student is ready for it. Thus, the discipline of practicing is one of the primary objectives that will lead the student to progress.

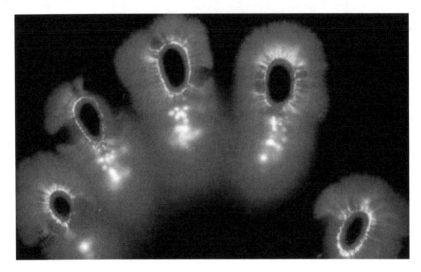

When the student succeeds to reach the result of 70% accuracy in the previous five decks only by using the psychic touch, which usually takes two or three months to complete, he/she is ready for the next stage.

Still, this is only the weaker manifestation of the third eye and now the student must work on the visual part of it, which is much harder to achieve.

STAGE TWO

In the second stage, training should be extended from three to four hours a day. After the completion of the first stage, average time to complete the second stage varies from four to six months.

The training starts exactly the same way like in the first stage, with the student's achievement of 70% accuracy only by using the inner sense of psychic touch. A new element, which the student has to add to the training, is focusing on the mental screen in a similar way previously described in the remote viewing process.

The student should become a passive observer and wait for the mental screen to become visible. When the level of concentration is reached and the mental screen is visible, the student has to change its location.

That can be done by using mental efforts to pull the mental screen from the location in front of the student's closed eyes to the back of the head.

Perhaps, in the beginning, the student will encounter some difficulty to achieve that, but with practice, he/she will succeed to hold the mental screen on the back of the head. The best way is to visualize that the mental screen has become transparent, to look for the counters of the table and to try to catch the rectangle form of the zener card, which is in the middle of it.

The most important thing for a student is not to forget to lose the psychic touch with the table behind even for a second. Both processes should be done in parallel mode, and the mental screen should be frozen in the right direction by the guidance of the psychic touch.

Next thing that the student should do is to try to observe through the mental screen towards the table where the card is. At the same time, the student has to free him/herself from all the other thoughts or emotions and to concentrate on the observation as best as possible.

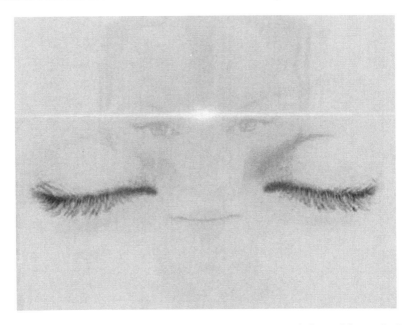

With the intensive concentration, the contours of the table and the card, which is on it, will start to emerge from the depths of the student's mental screen. The student's mind must be completely stable and frozen on those very weak counters appearing on the mental screen on the back of his head. The primary process in this stage will be similar to making a hole in the back of one's head.

The stronger the mental pressure on the back of the head becomes the stronger and more visible the mental screen becomes. By mental pressure, I do not mean physical grip of the neck or the head. I mean psychic pressure which is psychical 100 %, and which is a natural result of the strength of the mind reached by previous training with the zener cards.

In other words, the student guided by the psychical bridge between him/her and the table behind must force the mind with enormous amount of mental strength to make a psychic fissure in the back of the head.

The appearance of this psychic fissure is the first sign that the third eye of the student has started awakening. This period of training is very important because the actual thing that is happening is creation of the fissure in the etheric matter and the third eye will be learning to observe through it.

Anyway, the student will know when this fissure is present if he/she experiences these effects in the mind: Because of the major mental effort during focusing on observation through the mental screen in the direction of the table where the zener card is with the symbol up, one will soon feel that something has changed in his/her inner sight.

The darkness of the mental screen will be altered by some illumination.

Then, as the mental pressure on the zener card starts to hit stronger, it will become gray. Next, the gray color of the mental screen will start to express some foggy characteristics. Stronger concentration with the mental force through this foggy background will make the dot with less density visible on the mental screen. Finally, in this small dot something similar to a small fissure will start to appear.

Everything around this small fissure will remain foggy, but some light will start to appear in it. If the student continues pushing the mental force through this small fissure, he/she will realize that he/she is seeing something. At first, one will see unclear contours but in time and with practice he/she will develop his/her psychic observation.

Once the psychic fissure appears, the mind of the student must not become weaker not even for a second, but to keep the fissure open all the time. The fissure can also appear in some other direction like table legs or so, and the student should put some mental efforts to relocate the fissure directly above the surface of the zener card. It is very important not to become over-exited from the newborn situation but to remain perfectly calm, stable and focused on the training. In case the student becomes overwhelmed with excitement, starts to fool or jump around, the psychic fissure will close instantly, and the student will have to work twice harder to achieve the same level of development.

Very soon after the student freezes the fissure above the zener card, the symbol on it will start to become visible. However, in the beginning the images will be only black and white.

With further concentration on observing through the fissure on the mental screen, the color will start to appear. It will be coming slowly, but it will come. The moment the color starts accompanying the psychic sight of the student is a good point from which it will not take long before the student manages to scan all of the 25 cards correctly.

Perhaps, in the beginning through the fissure, some anomalies will be visible like seeing a square, which in reality is a circle, but they will vanish in time. Under no circumstance, the student should try to extend the psychic fissure until he/she has reached the score of 25 correct answers with five decks in a row. If the result is 24, it is not good enough and one has to work until he/she reaches the top score of 25.

Note: Jumping into the next stage of the third's eye development, without previously achieved perfection is a major mistake. Because of that, the student must be patient and wait until the result shows full readiness for the next level.

STAGE THREE

This stage covers the gradual extension of the psychic fissure and observation improvement. The training time extends from four to five hours a day. It is very important for the student not to miss a single day of training because the painstakingly achieved level of development is still very sensitive and it can easily retreat. Average time for completing the third stage varies but usually it takes two weeks to a month.

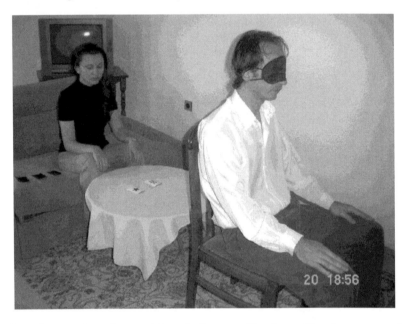

After the student has achieved the result of 100% of accuracy in minimum five decks watching through the tiny fissure, the assistant is allowed to put two cards at the same time in the middle of the table.

As before, perfection is top priority and the student has a chance to no more than just a single answer. Now, the assistant puts two cards on the table and the student has to put strong mental efforts to extend the psychic fissure for at least as much as to have both cards in his/her psychic sight. Soon, though maybe not at once, after the student succeeds to extend and freeze the psychic fissure, he/she will reach the result of 100% accuracy with two cards at the same time.

Because his/her inner sight will be constantly frozen on the surface of the table, the student will soon notice that from time to time he/she is able to catch the movement of the hands of the assistant.

In contrast to the previous experience, now the student can watch strictly in color. At this level, the fissure will allow the student to feel and watch in more subtle way. Although the third eye is developing very fast and the student is capable of feeling and seeing the next cards in the deck, it is advisable (at least in this stage) to concentrate only on the two target cards. Sometimes, the psychic fissure will get foggy but with the right mental pressure, it will get clear again.

When the student has managed to perfectly see the five decks with two cards, the assistant can add a card more and now the student has to observe three cards at the same time. As before, one has to use mental efforts to extend the psychic fissure even more, at least as much as to be able to have all three cards in the psychic sight.

Usually, this is the part of the stage the student achieves very easy, because now his/her third eye has become very active and the mind has only to use just some small mental effort to focus on the task and to solve it. The rule of five-deck accuracy with 100% applies here as well, and before achieving this result, one cannot go any further.

The moment the student has reached the needed result he/she is ready for nine cards at the same time. Now, the assistant has to put nine cards on the table in a formation of three rows with three cards.

Both the student and the assistant have to agree and clearly determine the rules of the next task. Whether it is going to be from left to right of the row or the opposite, or the first row is going to be the row closest to the student or to the assistant is completely up to them.

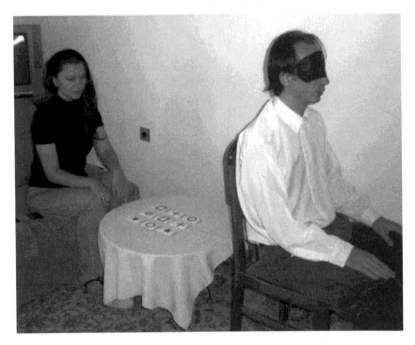

Again, using some mental effort, the student has to extend the psychic fissure, for at least as much as to have all nine cards in his/her psychic sight. At this level of the stage, the student has made a larger psychic hole and is no longer experiencing an observation through the mental screen, which is on the back of his/her head, but is experiencing an experience as if watching directly above the table.

In a way, the student's consciousness has departed very close to the border side of the psychic fissure and the student is watching through it.

Once the part with the nine cards is over, the student is ready for the fourth stage.

STAGE FOUR

When the student is done with the nine cards at the same time, put in a formation of three rows with three cards, the assistant has to put all cards on the table. It has to be in a formation of five rows with five cards.

Logically, bigger extension of the psychic fissure is required for the student to be able to see all of the 25 cards. It is different now, since the student now gains the ability to move the psychic fissure on his/her own will.

In this stage, the psychic fissure does not retreat and because of that, the student is capable to freeze or unfreeze it wherever he/she likes in the room. Soon, other effects will appear in the student's consciousness like hearing the assistant's thoughts, feeling of floating, all sorts of astral visions coming from the astral plane, etc.

All these effects in this stage of development have to be put aside and the student has to focus only on the observation through the expanded psychic fissure.

When the student has finished with all of the 25 cards in a formation of five rows with five cards with at least five decks, the next task is three rows, which contain 10 cards in the outer rows and 5 in the inner one.

To test the student's ability to perfectly see with his/her inner vision, the assistant should turn a few cards in different rows upside down.

The student has to locate the cards turned onto the other side and to tell which cards in which rows are with the black background up, with their symbols, of course. It will be a good checkpoint for both of them to get the real picture of the accomplished so far.

Watching through the black background of the zener card will not be difficult for the student at this stage. However, if it is, the student can solve the task only by using stronger mental pressure on the black surface of the card and the symbol will immediately become visible for him/her. As the training advances, the assistant should test the student's clairvoyance more often by putting harder and harder combinations in the rows like five circles in one group in the same row, or lots of cards turned upside down, etc., and to ask the student: "What do you see now?"

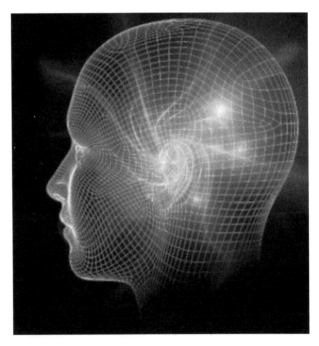

In other words, the assistant has to put the hardest combination of all of the 25 cards, but now, the student can do amazing stuff and probably, he/she will solve every task that the assistant assigns very easy and very fast.

Once they are done with the testing and the student does not miss any more, the assistant should go in another room and put all the zener cards on the floor.

To achieve the observation in the other room, the student has to move the psychic fissure through the wall, which separates the rooms and to freeze it above the floor where the zener cards are. When he/she successfully solves all 25 cards, the assistant should take a pen and point to different cards. Now, the student has to see in which row the card is, and normally, what is the symbol touched by the peak of the assistant's pen.

When all this is achieved, the student is ready for the next stage of the training. The time necessary for completion of the fifth stage varies from one to three weeks.

STAGE FIVE

In this stage of the training, the student continues to further develop the inner sight, and if everything goes, as it should, eventually, he/she will be capable to read with the physical eyes closed.

To complete this stage it usually takes 7 to 9 days. Before one begins with this stage, he/she has to repeat all of the previous stages. Since the student is now in great shape, he/she will finish them incredibly fast. I assume this so, because having reached this level of clairvoyance to repeat all of the four previous stages it will take the student less than 20 minutes. When that is done, the assistant should bring other deck of cards, which will contain all the letters of the alphabet.

By size and shape, they have to be the same with the zener cards with the only difference that where the symbols of the zener cards have been, the letters stand on the letter cards now. Just the same, as with the zener cards, the assistant has to reshuffle the letter cards well and to put one letter card in the middle of the table. The task of the student is to try to see the letter helped by the psychic fissure. The procedure is just the same, as with the zener cards. When the student finishes with 100% accuracy with one letter card in minimum five decks, the assistant can put two cards and when that also is completed, they can start with 3 letter cards at the same time. When they reach this level of the fifth stage the assistant can combine some shorter words like day, sun, one, car, etc. The student should not have any problems with the reading now, because his/her third eye is very active and the inner sight is very close to the clearness of the physical eyes.

Then, the assistant has to combine some four or five lettered words and when that is done as well, to start with more complex and longer words.

It is amazing for both of them to participate in live in this kind of event, and it is an unbreakable proof for presence of the pure mental power in the room.

The training continues with long and complex sentences, which will require other decks with letter cards because sometimes (for example) the letter E will repeat itself in the sentence more than 7 times.

Very important to be mentioned is that the student's consciousness will surely be exposed to all sorts of phenomenal effects like direct hearing of every assistant's thought, many astral visions that come and go incredibly fast, the loss of the physical feeling, etc.

The student will have to restrain from exploring those effects, which come because of the high level of the third's eye function.

Also, the student will experience a strong spinning feeling around the chair to the level that it will look like he/she is going to lose consciousness and fall into a complete blackness. The above normal mental power awaken by the third eye produces that effect and the student has to get used to it and to learn to control it.

Now the student's mind is very strong and the student will soon discover awareness of the processes that are running through his/her physical body never dreamed of before as possible to be sensed.

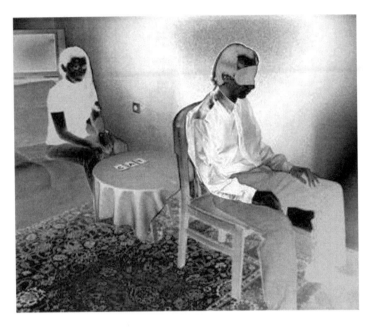

Stage 5

After the student manages to perfectly solve all the tasks assigned in the form of sentences to be read, the assistant should mix the two decks, the one with the zener cards and the one with the letter cards and put them on the table in many rows.

This time all the cards have to be closed or with the black background up, and the next task for the student will be to see them all. The assistant now has to take the notebook and record all the data the student tells.

The successfully solved task of this kind points clearly that the student is ready for the next stage.

STAGE SIX

In the sixth stage, the student will experience something as never before. He/she will be able to see exactly the same as with his/her physical eyes and much more. The student will achieve what most people consider impossible in this very advanced stage. However, before the student becomes capable of doing far greater extraordinary things, he/she will have to develop the inner sight even more by learning to observe deeper into the physical matter.

The stage begins with the assistant reshuffling the whole zener deck and putting it in the middle of the table. Now, the student is assigned another task and will have to see all of the 25 of the zener cards at the same time penetrating through the whole deck.

To achieve that, the student will have to change the frequency of the inner sight and to visualize all 25 cards placed in the astral space one above another.

When the vision of the whole deck levitating in the dark astral space in front of him/her appears in the consciousness, the student will have to use some strong mental effort to deeply penetrate through the whole deck.

He/she will have to tell the assistant the answers for all of the 25 cards starting from the first to the last one and the assistant should not touch the deck, not even once. The assistant will have to record the student's answers in the notebook and when all the 25 answers are given check the results.

It is relevant to be mentioned that this is a difficult task and in the beginning, the student will surely encounter some errors. That is because the student does not use psychic fissure but uses another frequency of perception instead. A little patience will enable the student to get used to this new way of seeing and he/she will surely learn how to do it.

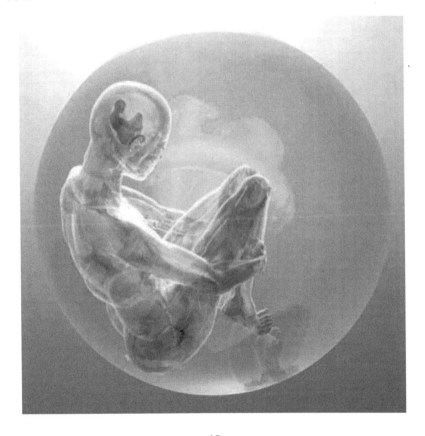

He/she can achieve the deeper scanning visualizing his/her astral hands removing and seeing one by one all the cards on the astral reflection of the physical deck, which is in the middle of the table behind. In other words, the student will have to visualize him/herself astrally picking one card from the deck visible on the dark astral space in his/her consciousness.

Then, turning it upside down the student has to try to see the symbol if it is not already illuminated and to throw the card away. Then, he/she has to repeat the same procedure with the remaining 24 cards.

When the student reaches the level with 100% accuracy with the deep scanning in minimum five decks one after another, he/she is ready for the next thing to be mastered. Now, the assistant will have to reshuffle the deck again and to ask the student to tell which card is (for example) 19th, counting from the top or from the bottom card.

To solve this task the student will have to reach again within his/her consciousness and to find the whole deck, which will be levitating in the astral space. Then, the only remaining thing to do is to count and when he/she reaches the 19th card, the student will have to remove it from the deck and to see the symbol on it. It is as simple as that and there is no other secret for this task.

The assistant will have to ask the student then about the symbols of the rest of the cards in the deck and when that is nicely done, the training continues with 2-5 cards at the same time. For example, the assistant can assign the student to tell the symbols on the 5th, 11th, 18th, 21st and the 23rd card.

Usually, when the student reaches this level of the sixth stage, the astral light will illuminate the symbols of the target cards and he/she will not have to count them one by one to solve the tasks. I have mentioned the way the procedure can be done anyway.

The next step in this stage is deep scanning through the deck of letter cards.

The procedure is the same as with the deep scanning of the deck with the zener cards. Once this is also accomplished, the assistant mixes those two decks into one and the student has to see them all starting from the top to the bottom card.

This is a very good exercise or should I better say test, and when it is completed the student is in a real good psychic shape.

The next level of the sixth stage is mastering the zoom ability of the student's inner sight. Including a book into the training should do the trick, so the assistant should put it in the middle of the table and open it on some page.

Then, the assistant will have to choose one sentence from the page and to encircle it with a pen.

The task of the student is to move the inner sight through the psychic fissure above the surface of the book and to start to zoom it until he/she reaches clearness to read from the page.

To pull this off, the student will have to work and train hard because maximum concentration and full control of the psychic fissure is required. The student will have to find out the number of the page of the book and to read the sentence circled with the pen.

When the student achieves this, he/she is capable of seeing so much clearer and better even to pull this off when the task of reading is in other rooms. In this stage, the student has to tear apart the psychic fissure by using the maximum strength of the mind.

In other words, to do that, the student will have to use ultimate mental efforts to extend the psychic fissure to infinity until he/she experiences that the psychic fissure is starting to tear apart.

Furthermore, he/she has to put final pressure until the fissure is torn apart completely and until the student gains an ability of seeing exactly the same as with his/her physical eyes.

Once the psychic fissure is torn apart, the student will see completely normal no matter to where the student points his/her head.

It is an amazing experience and only by using certain mental efforts, this new inner sight will be accompanied with other supernatural abilities.

This is a very high achievement of the student and his/her third eye is awake. From now on, the real effects of the astral force will start to appear and the student will have to learn to master them all.

STAGE SEVEN

The seventh stage is the most interesting. Further, the training continues with the student's practice to project him/herself into his/her astral body and to perform an observation in other locations. In this stage, the student needs two assistants to give the assignments, one to stay in the same room with him/her and one situated in another apartment.

The first thing that the assistant in the other apartment should do is to take one photo and put it on a table with the image up. Now that the psychic fissure is torn apart and the student watches with the mind just the same he/she would observe with physical eyes the student faces another task.

He/she has to leave the physical body and to take a short astral trip to the other apartment with the purpose to see the photo that is on the table. Then, he/she has to return to the physical body and to tell the first assistant all the data collected from the out of the body experience.

Both assistants should be in touch by cell-phone all the time during the seventh stage to exchange the data and clarify the accuracy of the student's observations.

The best part is that the time has come for the student to explore all of the psychic effects that have been coming into his/her consciousness a long time. Because of the great strength of his/her consciousness, the student is capable of leaving the physical body in less than five seconds.

It is enough for him or her to use some mental effort to astrally project at least two meters up front.

Then if one turns around he/she will find him/herself sitting on the chair blindfold. As soon as the student does that, the perspective of the inner observation changes, he/she will lose the physical sense and will find him/herself in a new body standing two meters in front of him/herself. If he/she looks upon him/herself, the student will see that he/she is in a transparent body, which is a complete copy of the physical carrier.

The student will also notice the tiny white line, which is representing the human contour and some smaller or larger blue illumination around it. The whole room will be perfectly visible to his/her astral vision and he/she will soon discover that he/she can see much better and deeper than being ever able with his/her physical eyes, of course if that is what the individual wants. Perhaps in the beginning, the student will experience biolocation because of not being experienced enough to hold his/her consciousness on the astral plane but in time one will lean to control the new, immaterial body.

Now is the right time for the student to learn to use the astral body, starting with a strong command to leave the apartment. As soon as he/she does that, the student will realize that his/her astral body reacts on even tiniest wish or command.

To reach the apartment where the second assistant is, the student can concentrate to find him/herself directly in front of the table where the task is and his/her astral body will teleport there immediately. It is also possible to do the same by the standard way of penetrating through walls, entering into other apartments, going out and flying until reaching the target apartment, etc. However, after the student has reached the target apartment, he/she has to look around and walk to the table where the photo has been placed.

It is appropriate to try to remember as many details as he/she can about the apartment and all the things seen on the way there and back, before he/she returns to the physical body.

After the student regains the physical feeling of sitting on the chair again, he/she has to describe the photo to the first assistant with all the data noticed during the astral excursion.

Then, the assistants have to compare all the data from the student's statement by their mobile phones. When the second assistant confirms the accuracy of the data in the student's statement, the first assistant is writing down the result in the notebook or a laptop.

The student has to repeat the same procedure by reading a sentence from some book, which will be put on the table of another apartment.

The reading should not be difficult for the astral vision of the student because of the previous experience with it.

However, it can take some time to master this to perfection. Then, the tasks will become increasingly difficult and chosen on the second assistant's free choice. For example, the assistant can put some thing in a closed box somewhere in the apartment and the student using the astral body has to find where the box is and what is in it. All the results will have to be constantly monitored.

A good exercise for the astral development of the student would be to work with both assistants at the same time.

Reading 10 digit numbers, one that will be in the same room in front of the first assistant and one that will be written on a sheet of paper in front of the second assistant is the content of this exercise.

The best test for the limits of the student's power will be to solve tasks that are very distant from his/her physical body by taking astral trips to other countries if he/she has some friend to assist him/her with the training.

Note: When the student has reached the level to read with his/her physical eyes closed and by using only the inner eye, the student will have to develop his/her mental skills more and more. In time and with practice these abilities will increase and the effects of the mental power will be beyond average human understanding. As far as clairvoyance is concerned, I will have to note that it is not complete until the third eye is fully open and active.

However, now the very advanced student who has mastered all these seven stages has also made tremendous step forward, but a long and unknown path still has to be walked ahead.

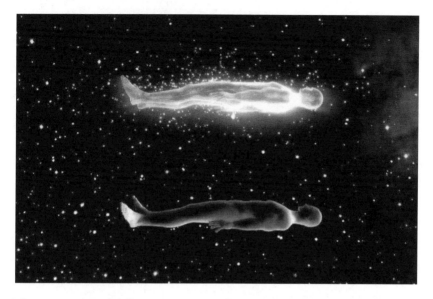

I have presented all seven stages designed for the awakening and developing of the third eye.

In this particular case it is the clairvoyance ability through the step by step opening of the psychic eye from which the sixth and the seventh are the most appropriate for developing many other psychic abilities like telepathy, psychometry, psychokinesis, etc...

For Skype consultations please contact: psionic.course@gmail.com

Or learn even more from the following books:

http://puretranquilitypublishing.com/the-awakening-life-force-energy/

CONCLUSION

It is essential for the human beings who wants to experience awakening and expand the frontiers of their perception, to become aware and understand the energies that run through their own inner energetic system. Without the knowledge of how to control those energies the progressive meditative states are not possible.

As mentioned, the Psionic Medium also known as Psionic Field, stands for the Infinitive Ocean of divine energetic substance that runs throughout the entire Universe. It is well known that the Medium is the intervening substance through which sensory impressions are conveyed or physical forces are transmitted.

As the vacuum of space cooled down to absolute zero of -273 degrees Celsius, a temperature where all matter should stop vibrating and emitting heat, everything was supposed to shut down.

However, instead of the expected absence of energy inside the vacuum of space, the scientists discovered the presence of an enormously huge unknown energy. Remarkably, it was coming from a completely non-electromagnetic source and it was initially called AETHER or Zero Point Energy (ZPE).

Research conducted by Dr Nikola Tesla led to his statement in 1891 that the AETHER "behaves as a fluid to solid bodies, and as a solid to light and heat", and that under "sufficiently high voltage and frequency" it could be accessed.

Note: Voltage is the electric potential difference between two points in an electric field. Frequency is the number of occurrences of a repeating event per unit time.

Tesla came to the conclusion that there is clear evidence of the existence of a powerful medium inside the very fabric of the Universe, which is used by unknown cosmic intelligence to move and distribute enormous amounts of energy, simply by accelerating electrons that further trigger the appearance of moving magnetic fields.

However, what the human brain is naturally capable of doing is beyond any technological devices that would require sufficiently high voltage and frequency.

Our consciousness can use this medium, no matter if we want to call it AETHER, ZPE, Psionic Field, Etheric Field etc., to travel, observe, send or receive energy or even teleport itself to different locations inside this medium.

The closest human terms that can be used to describe some of the dynamics included in this complex process that consciousness can use, are the terms "Remote Viewing" and "Astral Projection".

For a serious student of these arts, it is very important to understand that one of the ways that this works is that when the right conditions inside a human brain are formed, the consciousness can extend its field of perception.

In other words, when the correct brain frequencies appear inside the brain, due to specific mental effort of the consciousness itself, the DNA executes a command for a special chemistry to appear inside the pineal gland.

It starts producing natural Dimethyltryptamine (DMT) which turns on its higher functions. This immediately opens a small visual portal in the Psionic Field through which the consciousness can see through.

The moment it opens it creates a potential difference between two points inside the Psionic Field; the small portal that the pineal gland opened being one and the place of viewing being the second.

Thanks to this potential difference, the energy of the consciousness can flow or transport itself towards the secondary point which is the main subject of remote observation.

Which practically means, through the process known as remote viewing, the consciousness can observe places on Earth or beyond, that are thousands of kilometers away without the astral body leaving the physical body.

To observe places far more distant, the consciousness usually detaches from the physical body completely and travels inside its astral or some higher body.

Since the Psionic Field is an infinitive energetic medium that exists throughout the entire Universe, the way the human physical brain is genetically designed and interconnected, while in a deep meditative state, allows the consciousness through the power of its third eye to make a disturbance in the subatomic structure of the Etheric Plane.

It makes a small fissure in the fabric of this energetic medium, or to be more precise, in the exact region between the matter and antimatter.

It is through this small visual portal that the consciousness can penetrate the Psionic Field of planet Earth and beyond. At this stage, it is also important to understand that this Psionic Field is full of psionic energy that flows everywhere and is very sensitive to impulses that are coming from the living consciousness.

This psionic energy in its densest form is even running through our physical world and it is energizing the atomic particles of everything that we call "solid matter".

But the real magic of the Universe begins beyond the boundaries of the visible Universe.

Good luck on your astral journey through the immaterial Universe and always remember to use your new psychic abilities wisely.

If you use your abilities wisely and for greater good, there is no doubt that the experience of this magnificent journey, will one day make you realize that unconditional love is the eternal vibrational resonance of source consciousness that holds the fabric of the Universe together.

It will make you realize that the evolution of human consciousness is only possible through spiritual awakening. And then you will become a living light of divine consciousness, through which the divine cosmic plan will manifest and that powerful resonance will encourage other souls to step into the immaterial part of the Universe without fear and join the light.

Namaste,

Pane "AstralWalker" Andov

April, 2019

Copyright © Pure Tranquility Publishing 2019

Made in the USA
Columbia, SC
23 April 2022